T0383409

LOST IN REVERIE

AFA ANNFA · ANA MIMINOSHVILI · ANDREA WAN · ANXO VIZCAÍNO · BOBBY LEASH · CÉLINE DUCROT · JUN CEN · LISA MOUCHET · MARIE MURAVSKI · MICHAEL DANDLEY · NANCY LIANG · NICOLETTA CECCOLI · OWEN GENT · TAE LEE · XIAO HUA YANG · YIYI WANG

INTO THE DARK

ACKNOWLEDGEMENTS

We would like to specially thank all the artists and illustrators who are featured in this book for their significant contribution towards its compilation. We would also like to express our deepest gratitude to our producers for their invaluable advice and assistance throughout this project, as well as the many professionals in the creative industry who were generous with their insights, feedback, and time. To those whose input was not specifically credited or mentioned here, we also truly appreciate your support.

FUTURE EDITIONS

If you wish to participate in viction:ary's future projects and publications, please send your portfolio to:
submit@victionary.com

LOST IN REVERIE

FOREWORD
by JUN CEN

Dreams are fascinating. I am always curious about them, yet am never quite good at remembering them; which is why, instead of storing them as stories in my memory, I turn them into delicate dioramas that represent the scenes where the dreams take place. Every once in a while, I study these dioramas closely – like the one of a dream that I had when I was around 15. In it, I am sitting in the middle of a sunlit classroom with oversized windows, and the air is deathly still. The only sound to indicate the passing of time is the steady click-clack of high heels from the teacher walking along an aisle between the desks. When my attention turns to the classmate sitting in front of me, I find a flat human-shaped figure in place of a person, and it soon dawns on me that I am surrounded by cardboard cut-outs. Looking back, I was probably having a nightmare, but its overall aesthetic and the interesting setting that I was in remain etched on my mind.

Although I do not remember my dreams very well, it does not stop me from daydreaming. When do you usually daydream, I wonder? Personally, I find that music always takes me to a different dimension, as my stream of consciousness echoes the flow of the notes and the beats in the rhythm. Another activity that sets off my daydreams is my newfound love for taking long walks, during which I am also mapping an inner world. It is almost an instinct for artists to capture their dreams in art. In my opinion, good art not only resonates with emotions, but also creates space for imagination. When you are captivated by a piece of art, you create your own dreams.

What the art provides is a container or scene for you to put your content or stories in; and it is such an enchanting idea that one's dreams can evoke those of another.

As an artist, it is dangerous to stick to a single style or way of thinking, but by immersing myself in imagination, I find making art about dreams to be a healing experience. In a recent group meditation session guided by my friend, she told us to visualise our thoughts as an infinite number of bubbles and merely observe them 'coming and going' around us instead of trying to touch them. I realised later on that I was able to picture this scene so vividly in my mind because it resembled a short comic that I had done years ago, and it made me smile. In my comic, a girl in a dimly lit cave is standing in front of a gigantic bubble with her face in it. Around the gigantic bubble are millions of smaller bubbles, and upon touching one of them, she finds herself waking up in a spaceship. She walks towards the window as the spaceship flies by a colossal bubble-planet, and sees her face in the planet too. My friend loved this story, as did the people who resonated with the artwork on my Instagram account.

No matter how hard we try to understand them, dreams will always be mysterious. The harder we try to unveil their meaning, the harder the apparatus of the conscious mind works to inhibit us from diving deeper. Some have asked, 'what if in dreams, we have a glimpse of a parallel reality, while the lives that we live are just dreams?' – but to me, the fun lies in the assumption that artists are creating dreams within dreams.

"Would you tell me, please,
which way I ought to go from here?"

"That depends a good deal on
where you want to get to,"
said the Cat.

"I don't much care where—"
said Alice.

"Then it doesn't matter
which way you go," said the Cat.

— Excerpt from 'Alice's Adventures in Wonderland'
by Lewis Carroll

A SIMPLE GUIDE
TO GETTING LOST IN REVERIE

In this book, you will not find a Table of Contents nor page numbers, for—much like the Cheshire Cat's response to Alice who asks him for directions in Wonderland—where you end up really does not matter.

All you have to do is follow your instincts INTO THE LIGHT or INTO THE DARK, and see where the dreams take you, as you wander through the surrealistic realms of the artists and illustrators featured.

BEFORE SETTING OFF,
WE RECOMMEND...

(1) setting ample time aside for your thoughts to flow freely;
(2) preparing plenty of snacks or your favourite tea; and
(3) finding a cosy spot and a cat of your own for company.

Here's to the joy of discovering destinations unknown and losing yourself in the magic of the journey.

Marie Muravski

Pretty Princess

16" (40cm) Fully Jointed
Soft Vinyl Skin

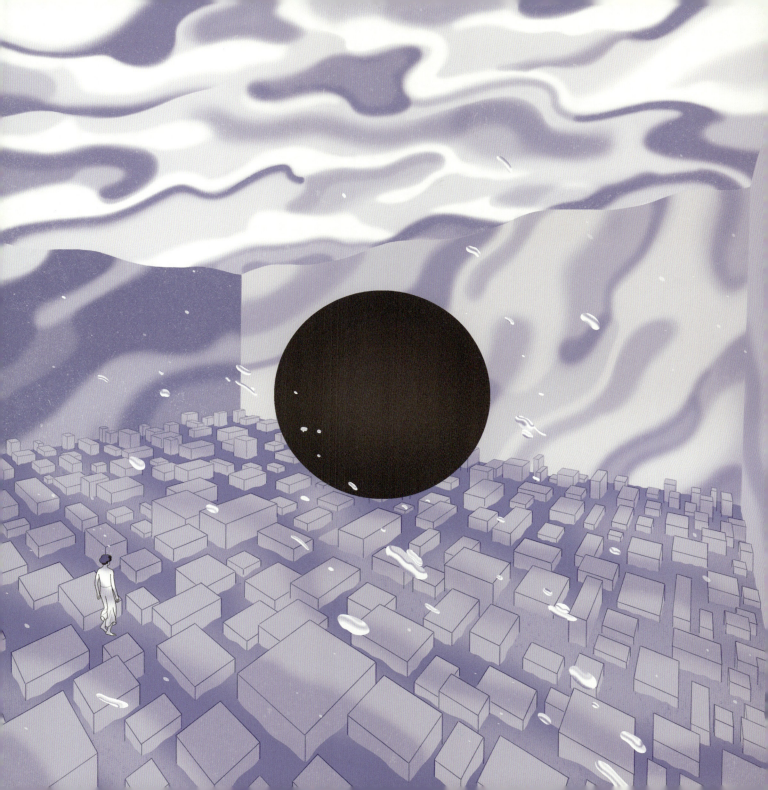

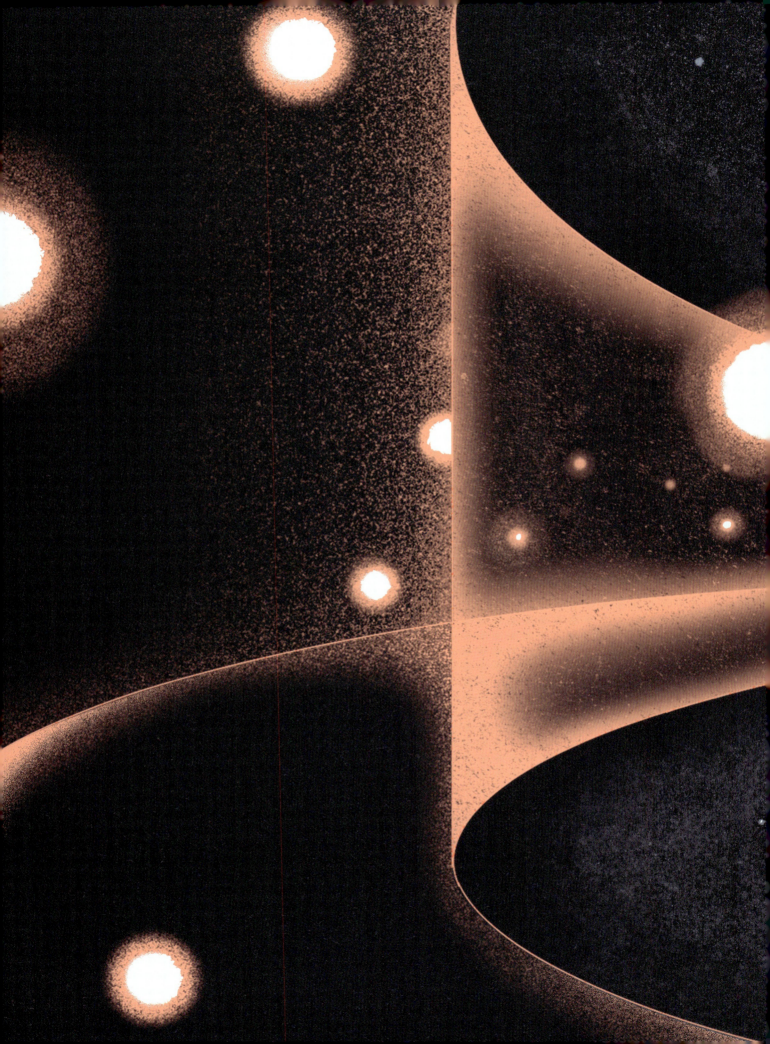

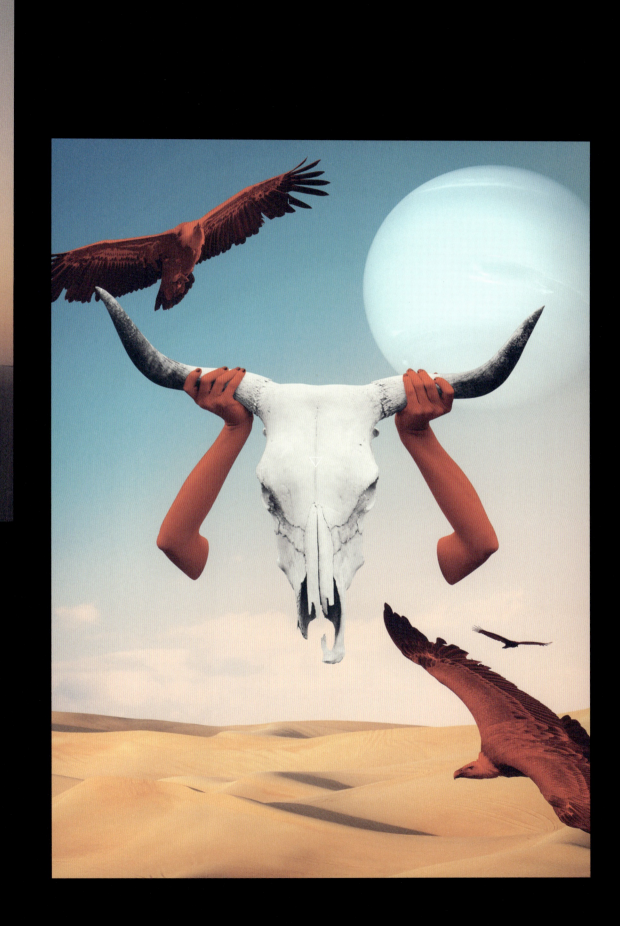

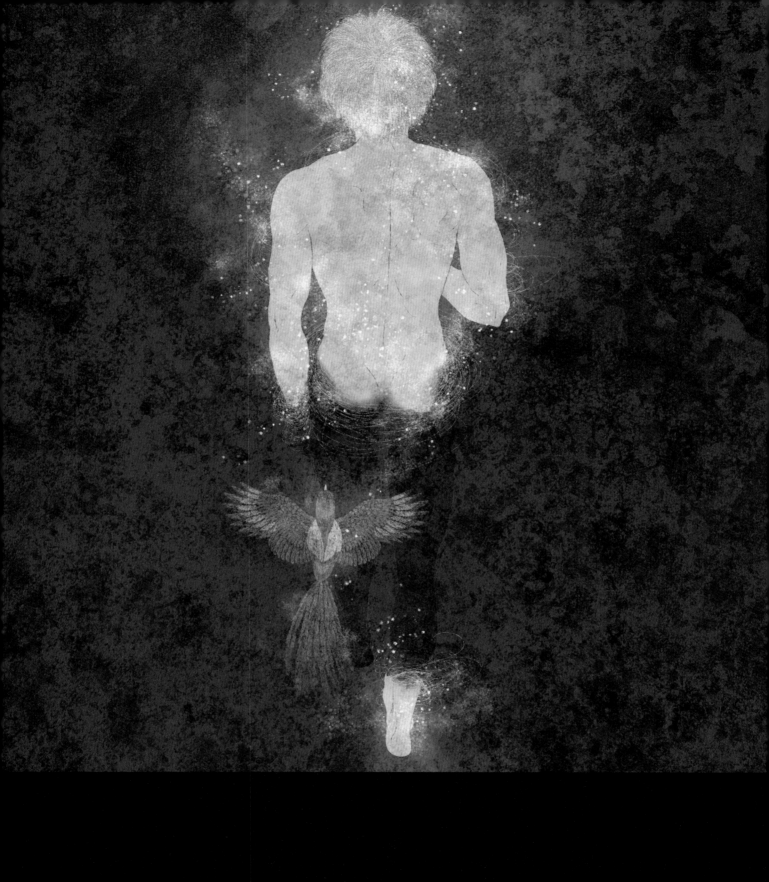

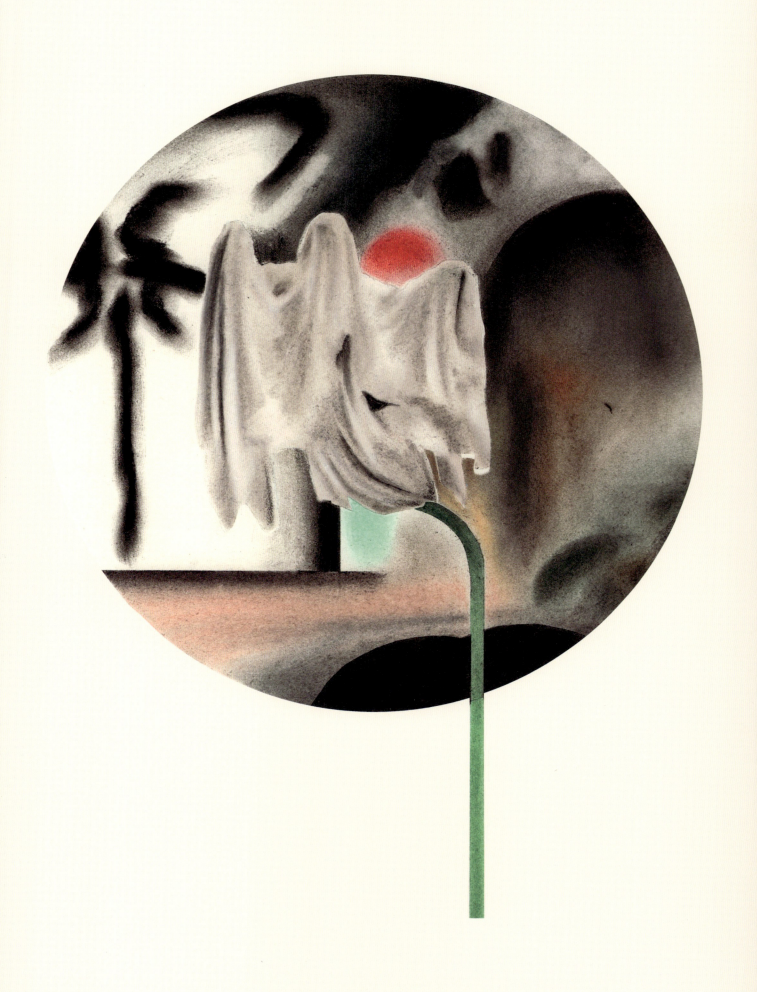

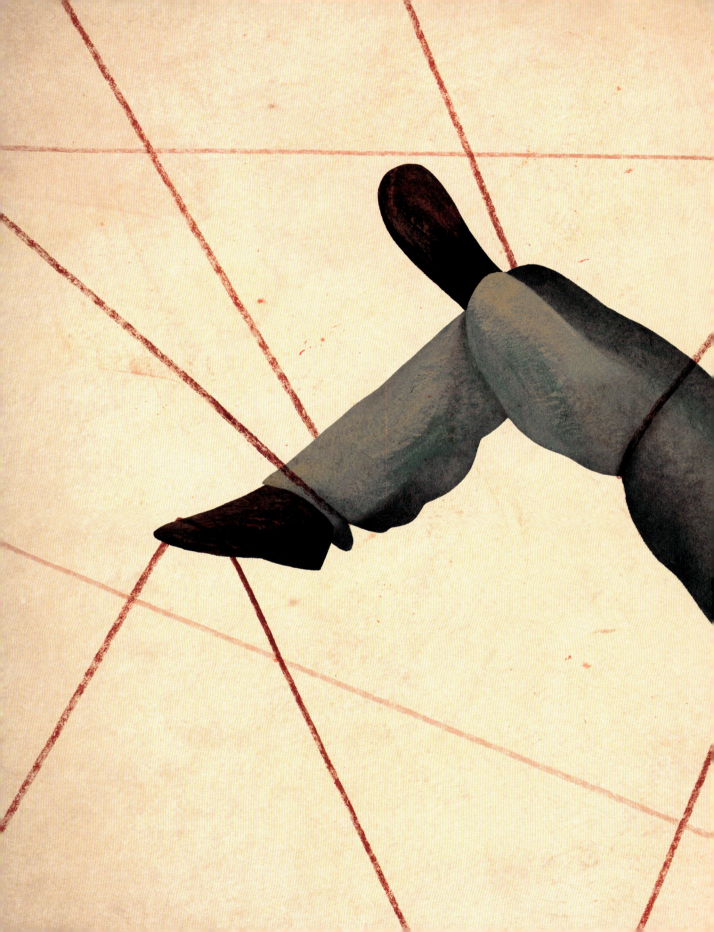

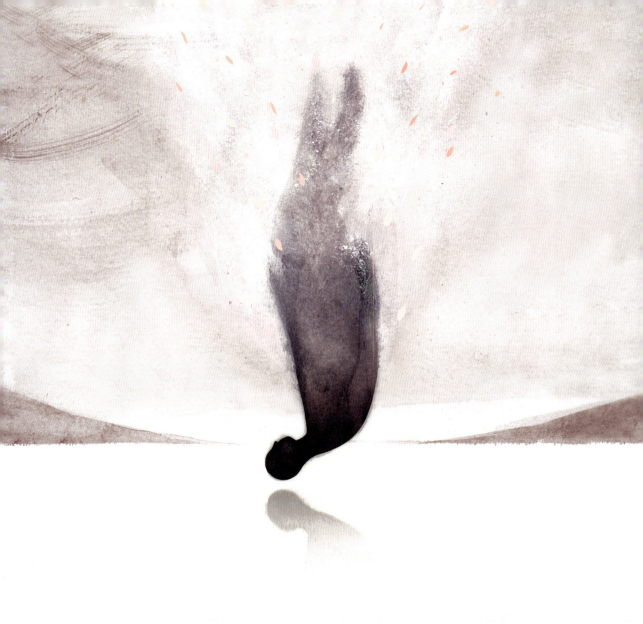

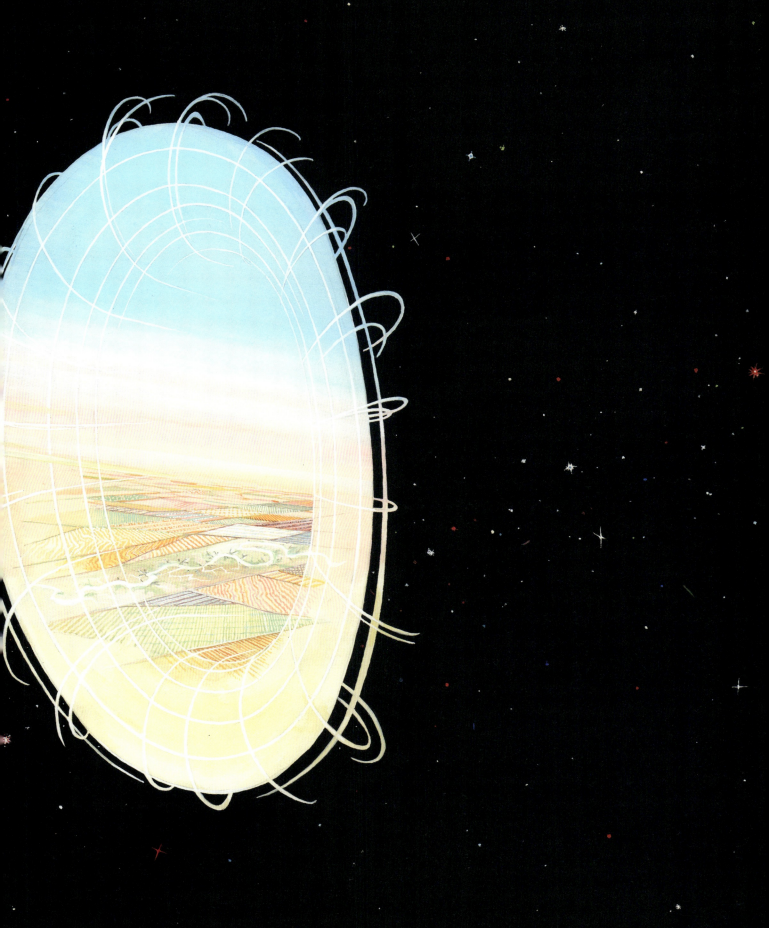

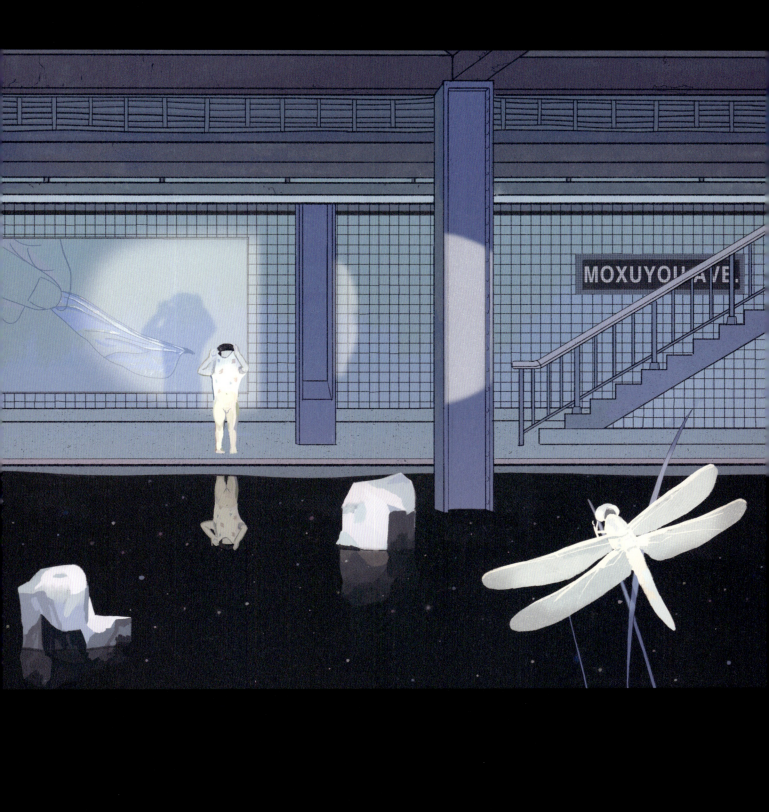

EPILOGUE
& INDEX

lying in my sleep

HE HOLDS
HIS FAVOURIT POSITION
IN BED
EVERY MORNING

HORIZONTAL

AS LONG AS
HUMANLY POSSIBLE

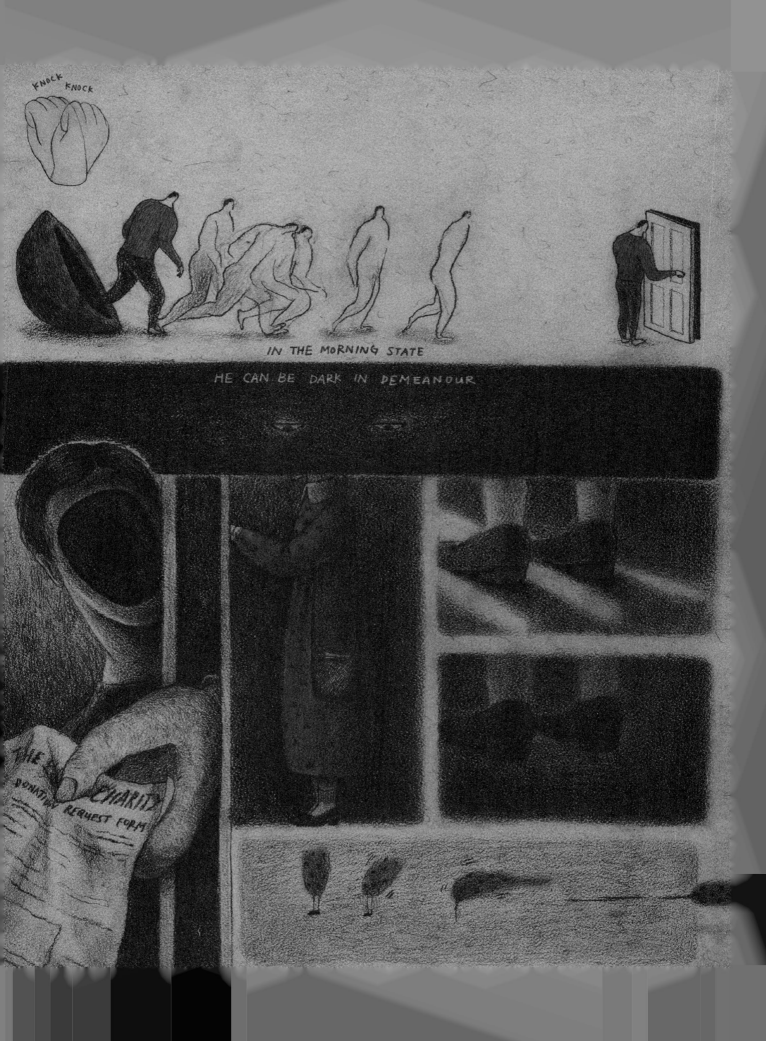

ONE HOUR LATER

SHE CHATS
CAUSE SHE LOVES TO CHAT

HE LISTENS
CAUSE HE DOESN'T WANNA BE SINGLE

so, how's your morning going?

just cooked a lovely breakfast

then this annoying charity person came by
oh really ?
did you give them any money ?
how much ?
oh... like... twenty pounds...
aw! sweet of you! honey!

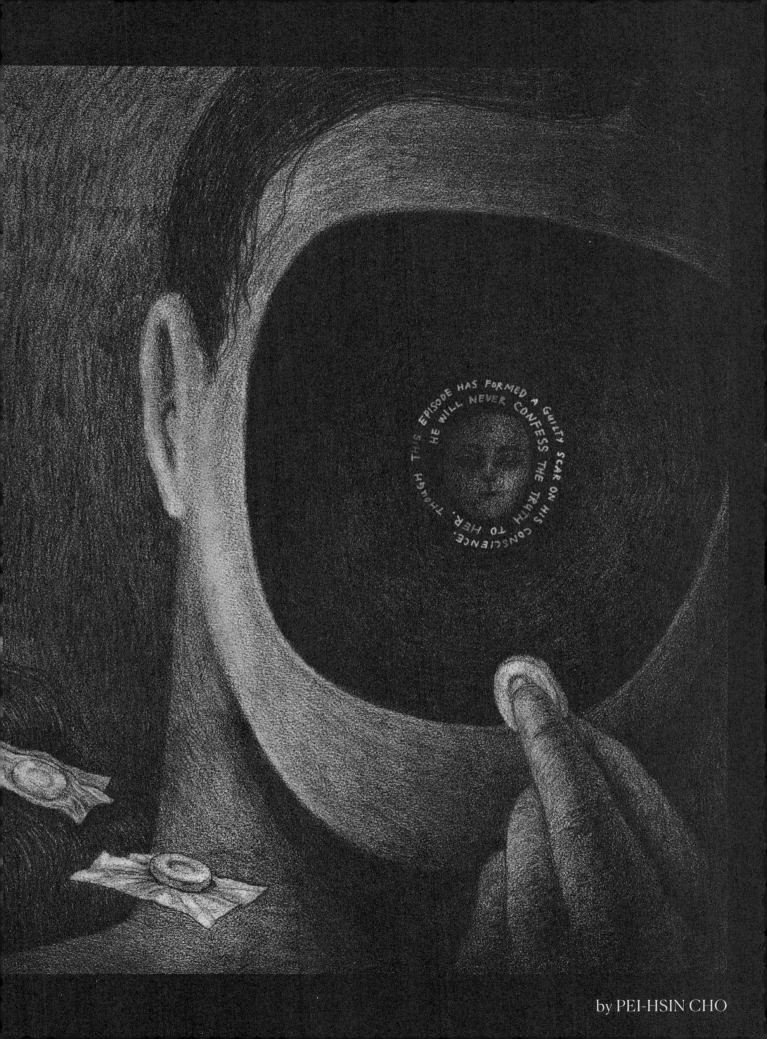

THIS EPISODE HAS FORMED A GUILTY SCAR ON HIS CONSCIENCE. THE TRUTH TO HER. THOUGH HE WILL NEVER CONFESS

by PEI-HSIN CHO

001
MOON WOMEN
Andrea Wan

Ink & gouache on paper
700 x 1000 mm

002
OPEN
Andrea Wan

Ink on paper
500 x 700 mm

003
**DANCING THE
DANCE OF LIFE**
Andrea Wan

Ink on paper
500 x 700 mm

004
**MALADAPTIVE
DAYDREAMING**
Andrea Wan

Digital
500 x 700 mm

005
**MALADAPTIVE
DAYDREAMING**
Andrea Wan

Digital
500 x 700 mm

006
**MALADAPTIVE
DAYDREAMING**
Andrea Wan

Digital
500 x 700 mm

007
**EXECUTION
GROUND**
Afa Annfa

Acrylic on canvas
995 x 500 mm
Special credit:
GUMGUMGUM

008
CONVERSATION
Afa Annfa

Acrylic on canvas
495 x 600 mm
Special credit:
GUMGUMGUM

009
HAIRY OCTOPUS
Afa Annfa

Acrylic on canvas
1520 x 1020 mm
Special credit: Keo.W

010
LOSING GIRL
Afa Annfa

Watercolour on paper
310 x 410 mm
Special credit: Keo.W

011
**THE INSUPERABLE
LONGING TO FALL**
Afa Annfa

Acrylic on canvas
Photo: Stephanie Kay L.C

012
STARRY DREAMS
Marie Muravski

Digital
300 x 400 mm

013
COMMUNICATION
Marie Muravski

Digital
269 x 339 mm

014
PORTRAIT
Marie Muravski

Digital
260 x 290 mm

015
DREAMS
Marie Muravski

Digital
240 x 310 mm

016
WRITER
Marie Muravski

Digital
260 x 360 mm

017
WHAT'S TRUE
Marie Muravski

Digital
210 x 307 mm

018
IN DISGUISE
Nicoletta Ceccoli

Acrylic on paper
400 x 300 mm

019
HONEY, I AM HOME
Nicoletta Ceccoli

Acrylic on paper
350 x 500 mm

020
INNER SELF
Nicoletta Ceccoli

Acrylic on paper
300 x 400 mm

021
SOFT VINYL SKIN
Nicoletta Ceccoli

Acrylic on paper
350 x 400 mm

022
THE KISS
Nicoletta Ceccoli

Acrylic on paper
300 x 400 mm

023
IN BALANCE
Céline Ducrot

Airbrush on paper
290 x 420 mm

024
IN BALANCE
Céline Ducrot

Airbrush on paper
290 x 420 mm

025
IN BALANCE
Céline Ducrot

Airbrush on paper
1350 x 1900 mm

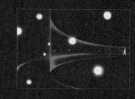

033
FACING DEATH
WITHOUT RELIGION
Jun Cen

Digital
406 x 290 mm

041
BLESSED TO BE
DEPENDENT
Nancy Liang

Drawing, handmade
textures, paper
cutting, digital
450 x 310 mm

026
CASINO
Céline Ducrot

Airbrush on wood
300 x 400 mm

034
THE BIRTH I
Anxo Vizcaíno

Digital
508 x 339 mm

042
OVER THE MOON II
Nancy Liang

Drawing, handmade
textures, paper
cutting, digital
400 x 400 mm

027
NO MORE SLEEP
Céline Ducrot

Airbrush on wood
1200 x 1600 mm

035
RITO
Anxo Vizcaíno

Digital
343 x 485 mm

043
OVER THE MOON IV
Nancy Liang

Drawing, handmade
textures, paper
cutting, digital
400 x 400 mm

028
TERESA
Céline Ducrot

Airbrush on wood
600 x 800 mm

036
TALES OF
ERRANTIA:
CHAPTER IV
Anxo Vizcaíno

Digital
322 x 479 mm

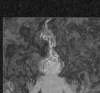

044
GENDER
DEFINITIONS
Yiyi Wang

Digital
500 x 500 mm

029
TEXT ME
Jun Cen

Digital
338 x 206 mm

037
TALES OF
ERRANTIA:
CHAPTER I
Anxo Vizcaíno

Digital
322 x 479 mm

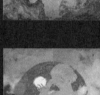

045
GENDER
DEFINITIONS
Yiyi Wang

Digital
500 x 500 mm

030
WHAT IT MEANS
TO LOOK LIKE ME
Jun Cen

Digital
352 x 313 mm

038
THE
OBSERVATORY II
Anxo Vizcaíno

Digital
400 x 600 mm

046
GENDER
DEFINITIONS
Yiyi Wang

Digital
500 x 500 mm

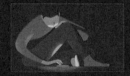

031
TEXT ME
Jun Cen

Digital
338 x 206 mm

039
THE
OBSERVATORY V
Anxo Vizcaíno

Digital
400 x 600 mm

047
GENDER
DEFINITIONS
Yiyi Wang

Digital
500 x 500 mm

032
INVISIBLE CITY
Jun Cen

Digital
330 x 330 mm

040
OVER THE MOON 1
Nancy Liang

Drawing, handmade
textures, paper
cutting, digital
450 x 310 mm

048
BRIDGE
Yiyi Wang

Digital
500 x 500 mm

049
BRIDGE
Yiyi Wang

Digital
500 x 500 mm

057
DON'T GIVE ME HOPE
Bobby Leash

Digital
508 x 635 mm

065
THE MYSTERY OF THE MIST HOUSE
Lisa Mouchet

Pastel dry
170 x 230 mm

050
JASMINE
Ana Miminoshvili

Digital
420 x 420 mm

058
NIGHTMARE AND WHY WE MET THERE
Bobby Leash

Digital
762 x 508 mm

066
DISCOVERY AND KNOWN LAND
Lisa Mouchet

Pastel dry
210 x 297 mm

051
EYEBALLS
Ana Miminoshvili

Digital
297 x 390 mm

059
ASTRAL EROTICISM
Tae Lee

Acrylic on canvas
610 x 819 mm

067
VACANCY OF A SPY
Lisa Mouchet

Pastel dry
420 x 594 mm

052
LADYBUGS
Ana Miminoshvili

Digital
297 x 297 mm

060
WITHOUT MORALIZING, WITHOUT HARSHNESS, WITHOUT DECEPTION
Tae Lee

Acrylic on canvas
406 x 508 mm

068
LAURENCE 666 - LE HUITIÉME
Lisa Mouchet

Pastel dry
205 x 260 mm

053
CATERPILLAR
Ana Miminoshvili

Digital
304 x 304 mm

061
INVISIBLE WAVES
Tae Lee

Acrylic on canvas
762 x 1016 mm

069
HERE ARE SOME PLANTS, MAYBE SHE KNOWS WHAT TO DO TO SAVE OUR LIVES!
Lisa Mouchet

Pastel dry
148 x 210 mm

054
BIRCH TREE
Ana Miminoshvili

Digital
297 x 297 mm

062
BOTTOM OF AN ATMOSPHERE
Tae Lee

Acrylic on canvas
546 x 622 mm

070
SAUDADE NO.1
Owen Gent

Water colour, found textures, digital
320 x 320 mm

055
ARE WE OK?
Bobby Leash

Oil on canvas
600 x 600 mm

063
WHEW
Tae Lee

Acrylic on canvas
495 x 610 mm

071
SAUDADE NO.2
Owen Gent

Water colour, found textures, digital
320 x 320 mm

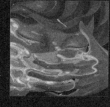

056
BRIGHT COLORED POISON
Bobby Leash

Oil on linen
305 x 305 mm

064
THE MYSTERY OF THE MIST HOUSE
Lisa Mouchet

Pastel dry
170 x 230 mm

072
STRUNG
Owen Gent

Water colour, found textures, digital
210 x 140 mm

073
FALLEN NO.1
Owen Gent

Water colour, found
textures, digital
300 x 300 mm

081
LAUNDRY ROOM
Xiao Hua Yang

Digital
229 x 305 mm

074
ASCEND
Owen Gent

Water colour, found
textures, digital
150 x 240 mm

082
UNTITLED STORY
Xiao Hua Yang

Digital
216 x 297 mm

075
**LEMONS &
NIGHTFALL**
Owen Gent

Water colour, found
textures, digital
220 x 140 mm

083
SEASHORE
Xiao Hua Yang

Digital
305 x 394 mm

076
BLOOM
Michael Dandley

Gouache on paper
381 x 609 mm

084
MOXUYOU AVE
Xiao Hua Yang

Digital
284 x 213 mm

077
FISTULA
Michael Dandley

Gouache on paper
431 x 558 mm

085
NEW ERA
Xiao Hua Yang

Digital
610 x 406 mm

078
SILENT CITY
Michael Dandley

Gouache on paper
304 x 228 mm

086
VR REHABILITATION
Xiao Hua Yang

Digital
210 x 297 mm

079
SHARD
Michael Dandley

Gouache on paper
508 x 660 mm

080
TERRAFORM
Michael Dandley

Gouache on paper
508 x 660 mm

DREAMERS OF THE DARK

AFA ANNFA
→ afaannfa.com

Afa Annfa is an award-winning illustrator and visual artist based in Hong Kong, whose work includes print ads, mural paintings, music video animations, magazine columns, smartphone apps, publications, and collaborative projects with different brands. She is a founding member of Eaton Workshop, a global brand merging hospitality with progressive social change.

007-011

ANA MIMINOSHVILI
→ anamiminoshvili.com

Ana Miminoshvili is a freelance illustrator and designer from Tbilisi who is passionate about crafting visual solutions. She loves playing with shapes, composition, and colour to create warm ambiences and combine geometric shapes with free natural lines.

050-054

ANDREA WAN
→ andreawan.com

Andrea Wan is a Chinese-Canadian visual artist. Having spent the last few years living in Berlin and travelling around the globe, she sees her creative practice as the container within which she harnesses her stream of consciousness. Her otherworldly images are reminiscent of dreams, fears, and thoughts buried within or shared.

001-006

ANXO VIZCAÍNO
→ anxovizcaino.com

Anxo is a freelance graphic designer, illustrator, and animator from Lugo. Consumed by unanswered questions about reality, consciousness, and mortality, much of his recent work is personal art in which he explores these subjects. His visuals are full of geometry and atmospheric backdrops, mixing different techniques such as photo manipulation, vectors, and 3D.

034-039

BOBBY LEASH
→ bobbyleash.com

Bobby Leash is a self-taught artist based in Bangkok. Cute, melancholy, and slightly macabre, his work is where the kids are ageless and play with the struggles of life and death.

055-058

CÉLINE DUCROT
→ celineducrot.ch

Céline Ducrot is an award-winning illustrator, graphic designer, and artist based in Switzerland whose works have been exhibited internationally.

023-028

JUN CEN
→ cenjun.com

Jun Cen is an award-winning Chinese illustrator and animator currently based in New York. An MFA degree holder from the Maryland Institute College of Art and the Overall New Talent winner of the 2013 AOI Illustration Awards, his work has been selected into the Society of Illustrators, American Illustration, and the Society of Illustrators Los Angeles, among others.

029-033

LISA MOUCHET
→ lisamouchet.com

Lisa Mouchet's work is often informed by her obsession with 'the house, the absence, and the objects around us'. To immerse viewers in the powdery grains of her pastel drawings or where the clues are hidden, she questions every visual element to feed her illustrated stories, just as an investigator would photograph a crime scene.

064-069

MARIE MURAVSKI
→ mariemuravski.works

Marie Muravski was born and raised in a small Siberian town in Russia. As a freelance illustrator, she collaborates with publishing houses and writers – travelling and living in different parts of the world along the way. She is currently focused on her family studio Voroch, which publishes picture books, indie games, and prints.

012-017

MICHAEL DANDLEY
→ michaeldandley.com

Originally from Massachusetts, Michael now lives and works in Zürich. His paintings ware 21st-century examinations of the landscape that explore cycles of destruction and creation that arise from environments interacting with human development.

076-080

NANCY LIANG
→ be.net/nliang

Nancy Liang is an Australian artist who focuses on tales of urban landscapes and sleepy places in suburbia. Her practice lies in between the traditional and the digital; employing drawing, hand-painted textures and paper-cut techniques that are presented through digital mediums such as animation.

040-043

NICOLETTA CECCOLI
→ nicolettaceccoli.com

Nicoletta Ceccoli lives and works in the Republic of San Marino. An animation graduate from the State Institute of Art in Urbino, she has been illustrating for children's books since 1995. Her work manifests a universe wherein everything that is beautiful is wounded. With soft starkness, she highlights the brutality and muddled nature of the transition of girlhood to womanhood.

018-022

OWEN GENT
→ owengent.com

Owen Gent is an artist and illustrator based in Bristol.

070-073

TAE LEE
→ IG: @taelien

Tae Lee is an artist working out of Los Angeles whose work focuses on ruminating on esoteric worlds – investigating the thin veil between consensus reality and a more enigmatic realm. Believing that separateness is an illusion, he embraces non-duality to allow the universe to unfold.

059-063

XIAO HUA YANG
→ yxhart.me / IG: @dawnwatch

Xiao Hua Yang is originally from Shanghai and now based in New York. His work has been recognised by the Society of Illustrators, American Illustrations, Association of Illustrators, 3x3 Magazine, Creative Quarterly, and Applied Arts Magazine. His illustrious client list includes The New York Times, The New Yorker, Wall Street Journal, SeatGeek, and Surf Twenty Magazine.

081-086

YIYI WANG
→ be.net/yiyiwangSKD

Yiyi Wang is an independent Chinese illustrator based in Chengdu, whose photorealistic paintings revolve around creative concepts that can move people's hearts.

044-049

DREAMERS OF THE LIGHT

066-071

...drawings, creating seamless painting-esque art pieces with new enchanted narratives that mash fictional elements from the medieval fantasy world and historical references with 21st century visual puns.

PO-HSUN HUANG
→ IG: @moo_dan_studio

Po-Hsun Huang lives and works in Taiwan. Driven by the concept of feeling 'abundant yet lonely,' he sets out to clarify reality from illusion through the materials he uses in his art pieces, creating a wonderland with elements that are overlapping, rebuilt, dissolved, and reconstructed.

001-006

RUNE FISKER
→ runefisker.com

Rune Fisker is a Copenhagen-based artist and illustrator. His abstract, surrealist style plays with geometry, line, and tone. The results are subconscious scenes where characters of distorted proportions entangle with phantom backdrops hinged between fiction and reality.

072-076

SHUKU NISHI
→ nishishuku.net

Shuku Nishi is an illustrator and a painter based in Japan. Her work has been featured in various media including books, advertisements, TV commercials, CD covers, and packaging. Taking inspiration from nature, she also creates block prints, oil paintings, and 3D works.

054-058

VICKI LING
→ vickiling.com

Vicki Ling is a Chinese artist and illustrator currently based in Chicago. Through her art, she demonstrates a strong eye for detail and a unique ability to convey emotion through her fictional imagery. An MFA holder in fine art from Central Saint Martins in London, she has worked with various clients and exhibited internationally.

055-059

WHOOLI CHEN
→ be.net/whoolichen

Whooli Chen is an illustrator based in Taiwan. A cat lover and a heavy reader with an affection for plants and animals, her art is immersed in surrealism, dream interpretation, Asian traditional art, and gentle colours.

012-015

HEATHER SUNDQUIST HALL
→ heathersundquist.com

Heather Sundquist Hall is an illustrator based in Texas. Her paintings are drawn from memories and often focuses on the details – whether it is the shift in light during sunsets she pays homage to, or the kind of plaid her grandmother's couch was in 1986. These details help her to illuminate nostalgia through new eyes.

016-020

HOI CHAN
→ hoichan.com

Hoi Chan is a Hong Kong-born, US-based illustrator who is always looking for the balance between nature and urban life; and how finding this balance translates into shapes and colours. His clients include The New York Times, The Washington Post, CBS News, Quartz, and The California Sunday Magazine.

050-054

JUNGHO LEE
→ leejungho.com

Jungho Lee studied graphic design at the Hongik University in Seoul. Since completing his undergraduate programme, he has worked as an illustrator for various clients in different fields. He is currently focused on publications and making his own picture book.

028-033

PEI-HSIN CHO
→ peihsincho.com

Pei-Hsin Cho is a Taiwanese visual storyteller with a particular focus on illustration and animation. Currently based in Berlin, her narrative-based work challenges storytelling possibilities, combining traditional and digital mediums to create delicate and atmospheric outcomes.

039-045

PETRA ERIKSSON
→ petraeriksson.com

Petra Eriksson is an artist and illustrator originally from Sweden, and currently based in Barcelona. She plays with colour and a mix of organic and graphic shapes in her work.

082-086

PHANTASIEN
→ IG: @__phantasien

Anindya Anugrah (a.k.a. Phantasien) is a self-taught illustrator based in Jakarta. Her unique approach involves making collages from public domain materials and combining them with her...

AKIRA KUSAKA
→ akirakusaka.com

Akira Kusaka is a freelance illustrator and graphic designer based in Osaka. Using only Photoshop, he draws for advertisements, book covers, children's picture books, web design, and the like. When he is not working, he plays the trombone in a two-man poetry, picture, and music project called 'Repair'.

044-049

CHING-YAN LAI
→ IG: @siuloy

Ching-Yan Lai is an illustrator based in Hong Kong who draws and paints in her spare time. She enjoys sketching outdoors, where she spends time silently observing the environment she is in, and at the same time, finding inspiration for her next painting.

077-081

DANIEL LIÉVANO
→ lifeisanillusion.com

As an editorial illustrator, Daniel Liévano has devoted most of his work to the creation of conceptual images for clients such as The New Yorker, The Economist, The Sunday Times, The Washington Post, and The Boston Globe. As an author, he is deeply inspired by his interests in semiotics, linguistics, and any other manifestation of the broader meaning of language.

060-065

FUCO UEDA
→ fucoueda.com

Born in 1979 and currently based in Tokyo, Fuco Ueda graduated from the Tokyo Polytechnic University of Arts Graduate School in 2003. Exhibited internationally, her paintings are done in acrylics and powdered mineral pigments on paper, cloth or wood.

007-011

GUY BILLOUT
→ graphis.com/portfolio/1/guy-billout

Born in 1941, Guy Billout is a French artist and illustrator with a clean and spare aesthetic style that sometimes incorporates an ironic element. His work has been featured in Atlantic Monthly magazine and several notable publications.

021-027

049
SOMEWHERE, NOT HERE.
Akira Kusaka

Digital
210 x 297 mm

057
HIDDEN AND EXPOSED
Vicki Ling

Graphite on paper
300 x 300 mm

065
HARP
Daniel Liévano

Digital
297 x 420 mm
Art direction & editing:
George Anderson Lozano

050
SELF PORTRAIT
Hoi Chan

Digital, pastel
420 x 420 mm

058
THE PLASTIC BLOOM
Vicki Ling

Graphite & colour pencil on paper
300 x 400 mm

066
VOYAGE
Phantasien

Digital
300 x 300 mm

051
GONE
Hoi Chan

Digital, pastel
362 x 420 mm

059
THE PLASTIC BLOOM
Vicki Ling

Graphite & colour pencil on paper
300 x 400 mm

067
DREAMFLOWERS
Phantasien

Digital
300 x 300 mm

052
FADING AWAY
Hoi Chan

Digital, pastel
431 x 303 mm

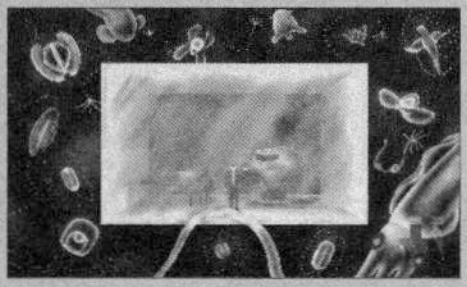

060
MANTO DE LA VIDA
Daniel Liévano

Digital
297 x 420 mm

068
MIDNIGHT AT THE OASIS
Phantasien

Digital
300 x 300 mm

053
SURVIVAL MODE IS OVER
Hoi Chan

Digital, pastel
362 x 219 mm
Art direction: Jovanna Tosello

061
BALLERINA
Daniel Liévano

Digital
297 x 420 mm
Art direction & editing:
Elena Becker-Barroso

069
SIESTA
Phantasien

Digital
420 x 297 mm

054
SALARY VS HOURLY
Hoi Chan

Digital, pastel
420 x 263 mm
Art direction: Emma Murray

062
WINDOW
Daniel Liévano

Digital
297 x 420 mm

070
SATURN
Phantasien

Digital
590 x 420 mm

055
DETACHED
Vicki Ling

Graphite on paper
230 x 300 mm

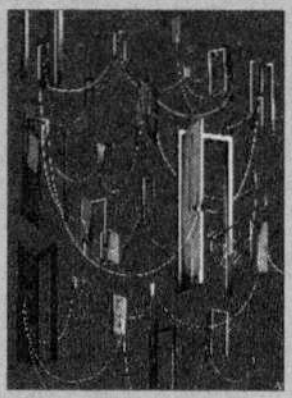

063
DOORS OF PERCEPTION
Daniel Liévano

Digital
297 x 420 mm
Art direction & editing:
Elena Becker-Barroso

071
SUGAR MOUNTAIN DREAMS
Phantasien

Digital
530 x 400 mm

056
HIDDEN AND EXPOSED
Vicki Ling

Graphite on paper
300 x 300 mm

064
TREES
Daniel Liévano

Digital
297 x 420 mm
Art direction & editing:
George Anderson Lozano

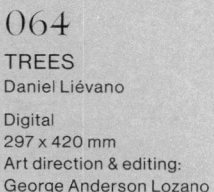

072
BETWEEN THE WALLS
Rune Fisker

Digital
297 x 420 mm

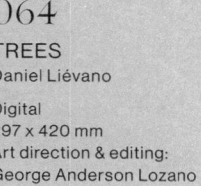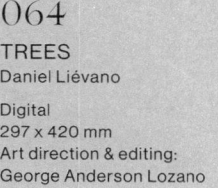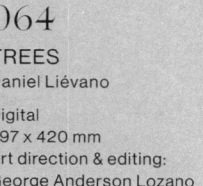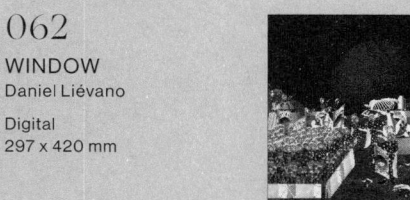

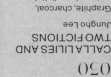

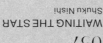

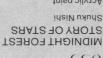
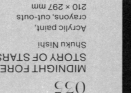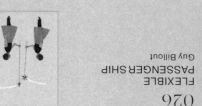
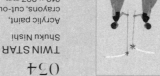
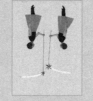

      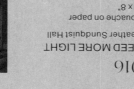 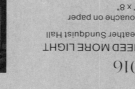

024
EVENING NEWS
Guy Billout

016
NEED MORE LIGHT
Heather Sundquist Hall
Gouache on paper
8" x 8"

008
COMMUNICATION
Fuco Ueda
Acrylic & shell white
on canvas
335 x 455 mm

 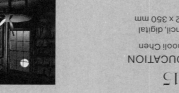 

025
MIDNIGHT
Guy Billout

015
EDUCATION
Whooli Chen
Pencil, digital
262 x 350 mm

007
SYMBIOSIS 2017
Fuco Ueda
Acrylic & shell white
on canvas
1300 x 895 mm

  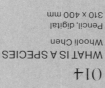 

022
THE CHILDHOOD
OF HERCULES
Guy Billout

014
WHAT IS A SPECIES
Whooli Chen
Pencil, digital
310 x 400 mm

006
DREAMS IN
SUMMER NIGHTS
Po-Hsun Huang
Acrylic on canvas
450 x 650 mm

  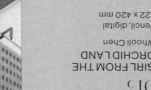 

021
TWO EXECUTIVES
& SHADOW
Guy Billout

013
GIRL FROM THE
ORCHID LAND
Whooli Chen
Pencil, digital
322 x 420 mm

005
WHAT WE HAVE,
CHERISH, AND
MEMORIZE
Po-Hsun Huang
Acrylic on canvas
1200 x 900 mm

    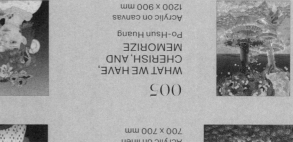

020
LONELY
PLANET JOY
Heather Sundquist Hall
Gouache on paper
6" x 8"

012
CITY LIFE
Whooli Chen
Pencil, digital
318 x 420 mm

004
BEFORE THE
BEGINNING, AFTER
THE ENDING
Po-Hsun Huang
Acrylic on linen
700 x 700 mm

019
HAY TV
Heather Sundquist Hall
Gouache on paper
6" x 8"

011
TO FALL ASLEEP
Fuco Ueda
Acrylic & shell white
on canvas
530 x 652 mm

003
THE OLD PLACE
Po-Hsun Huang
Acrylic on canvas
1000 x 800 mm

018
WHAT YOU WILL
Heather Sundquist Hall
Gouache on paper
8" x 11"

010
INNER GARDEN
Fuco Ueda
Acrylic & shell white
on canvas
1000 x 803 mm

002
ABOUT THE
REUNION
Po-Hsun Huang
Acrylic on canvas
800 x 1000 mm

     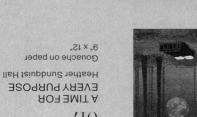  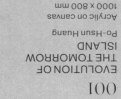

017
A TIME FOR
EVERY PURPOSE
Heather Sundquist Hall
Gouache on paper
9" x 12"

009
DREAM
WHEREABOUTS
Fuco Ueda
Acrylic & shell white
on canvas
420 x 297 mm

001
EVOLUTION OF
THE TOMORROW
ISLAND
Po-Hsun Huang
Acrylic on canvas
1000 x 800 mm

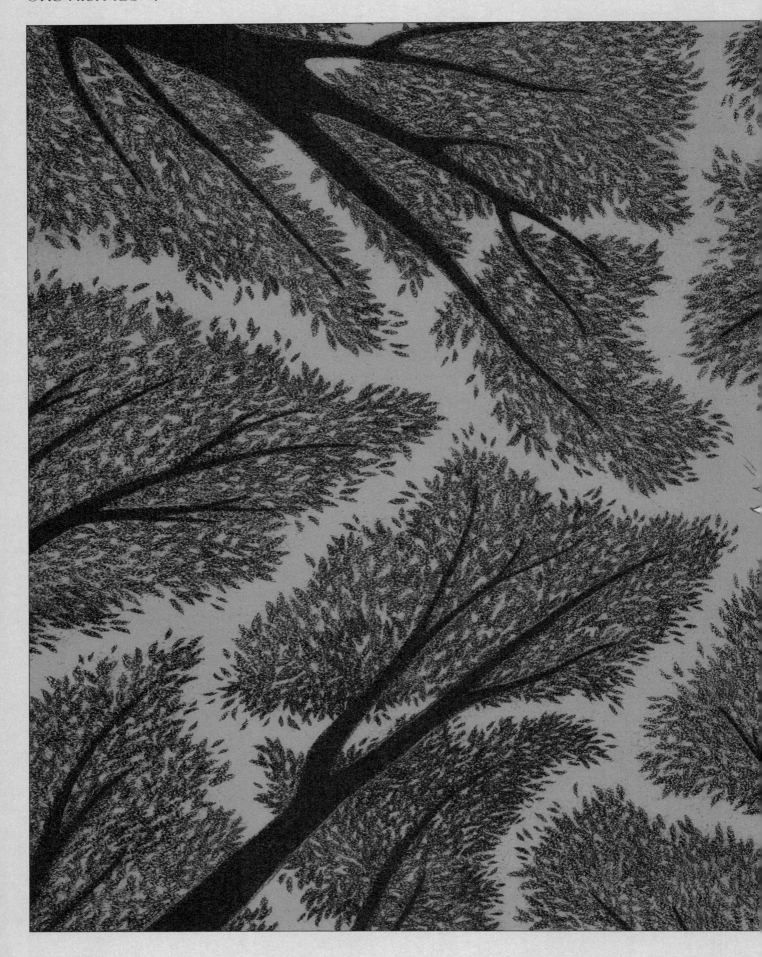

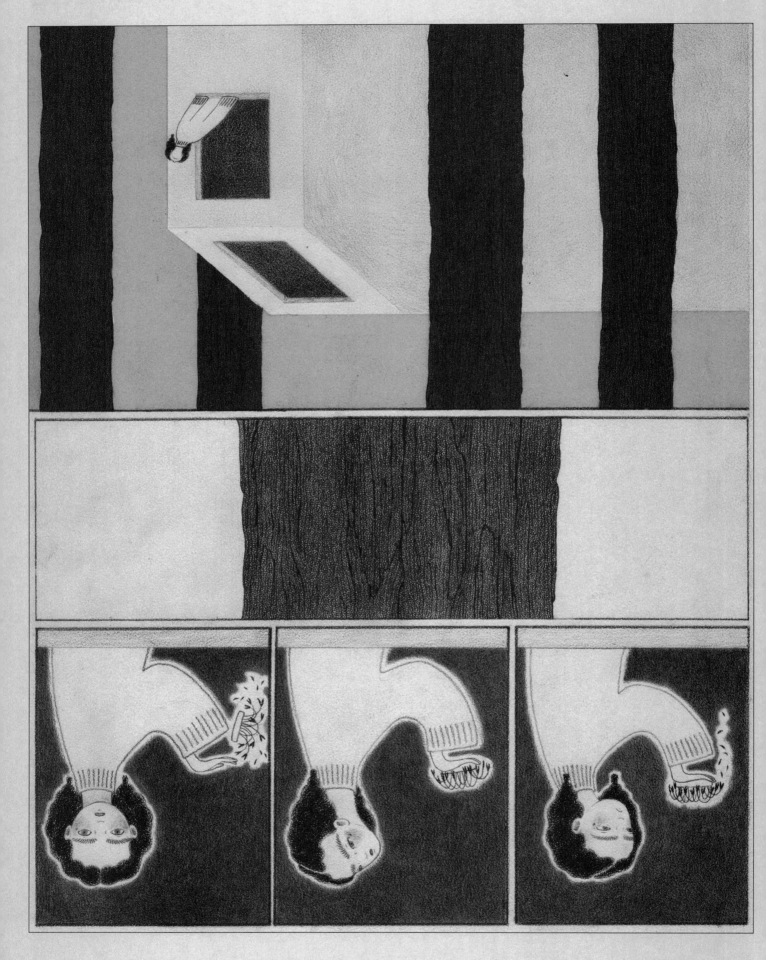

EPILOGUE & INDEX

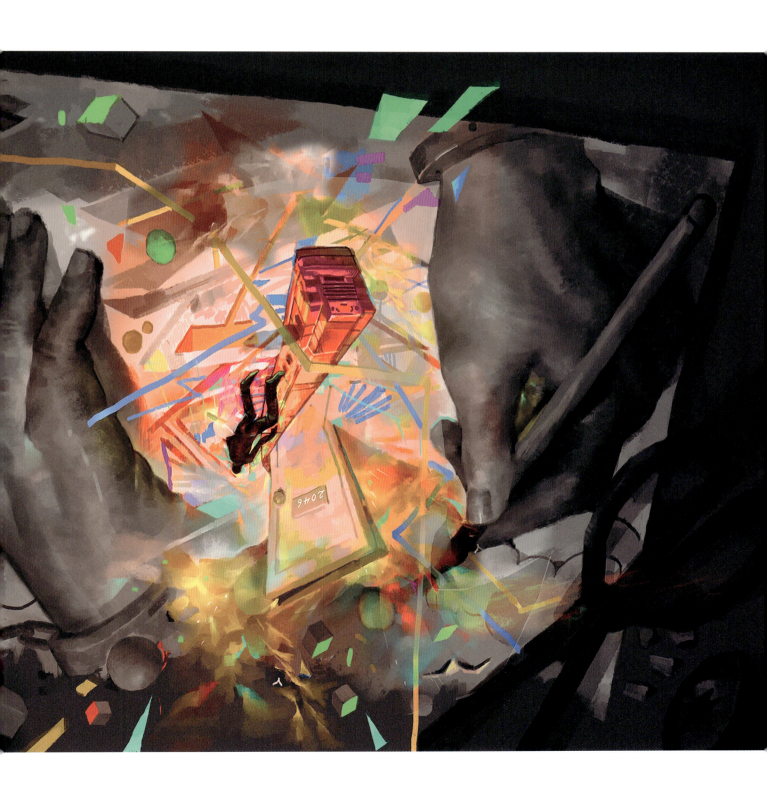

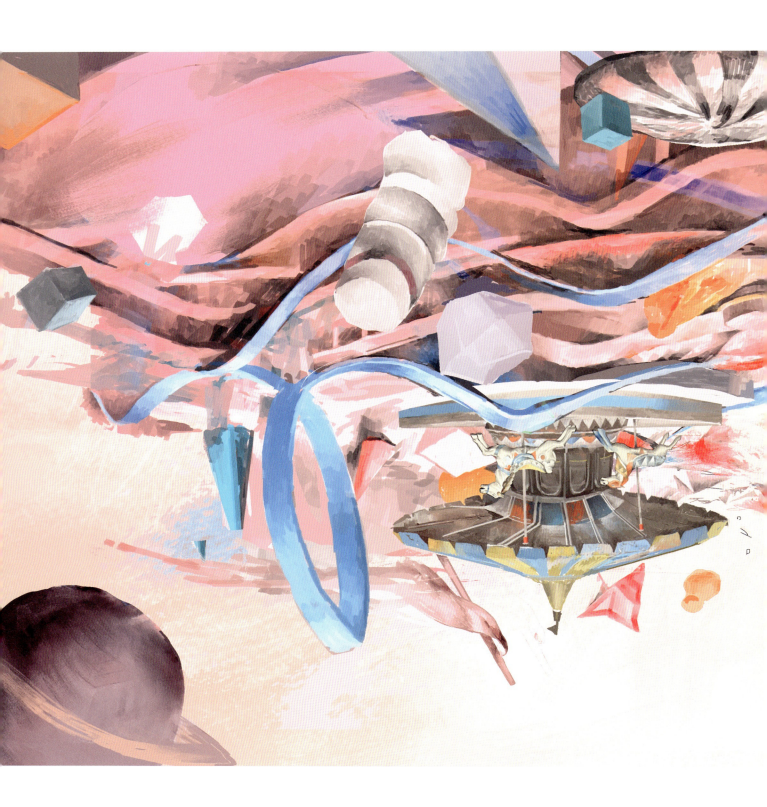

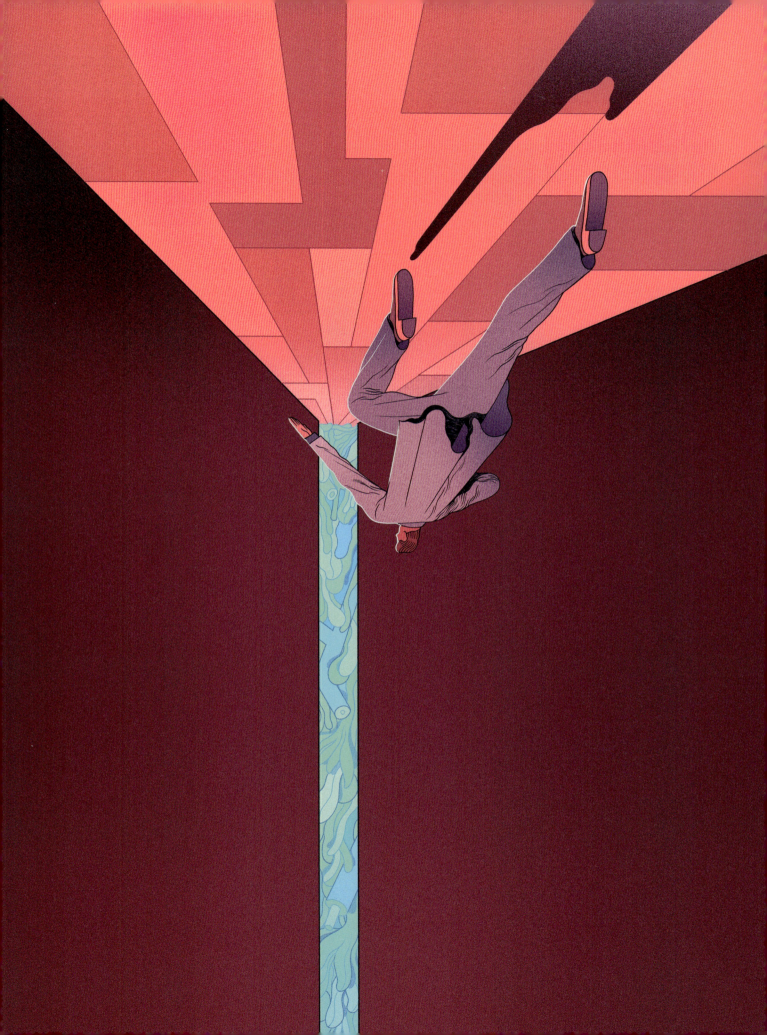

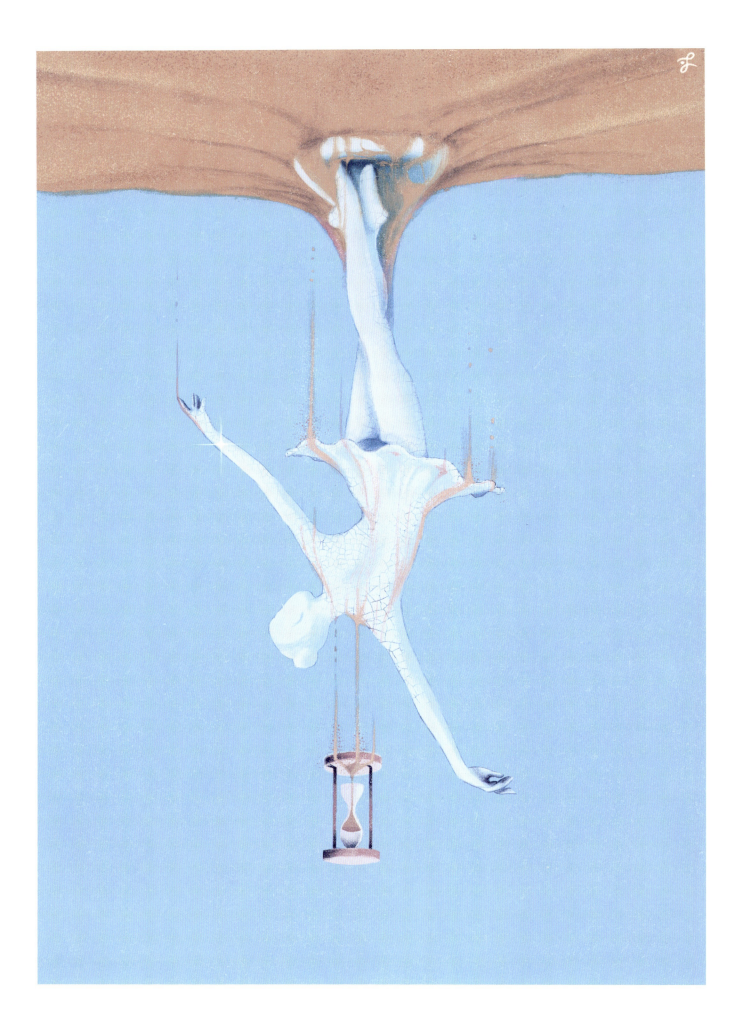

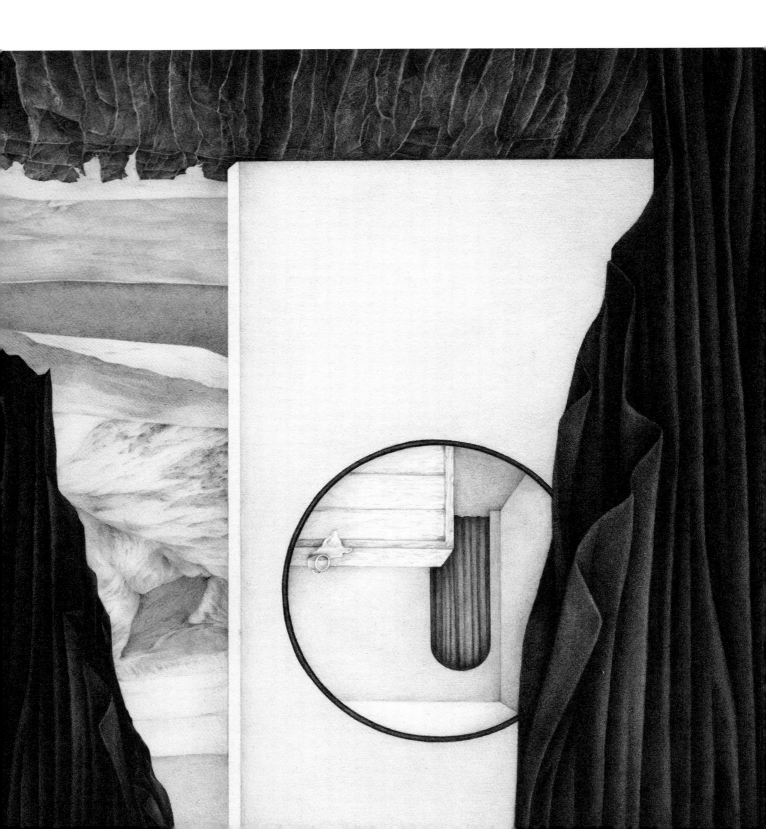

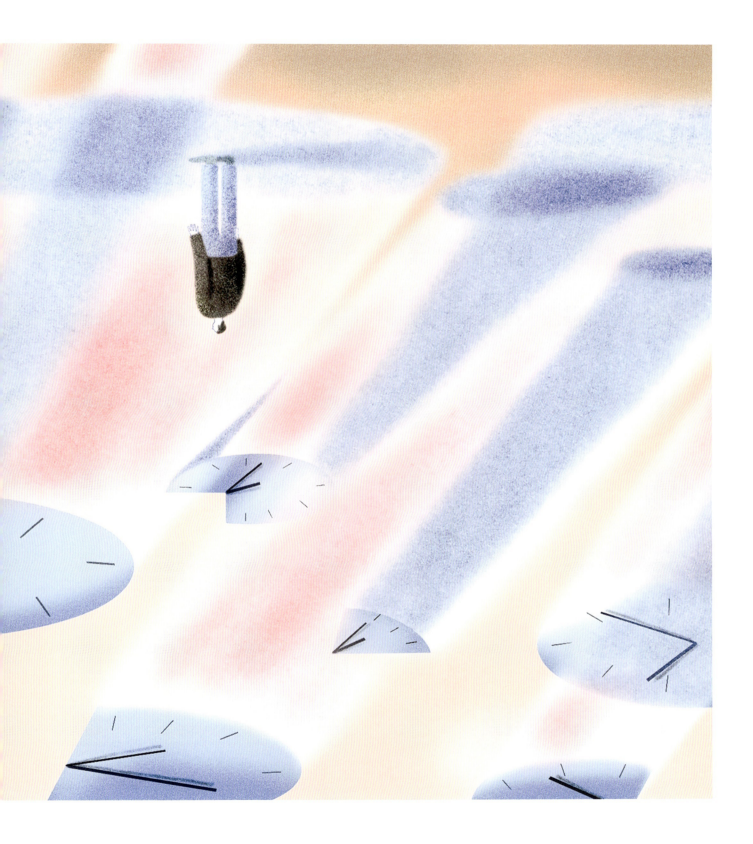

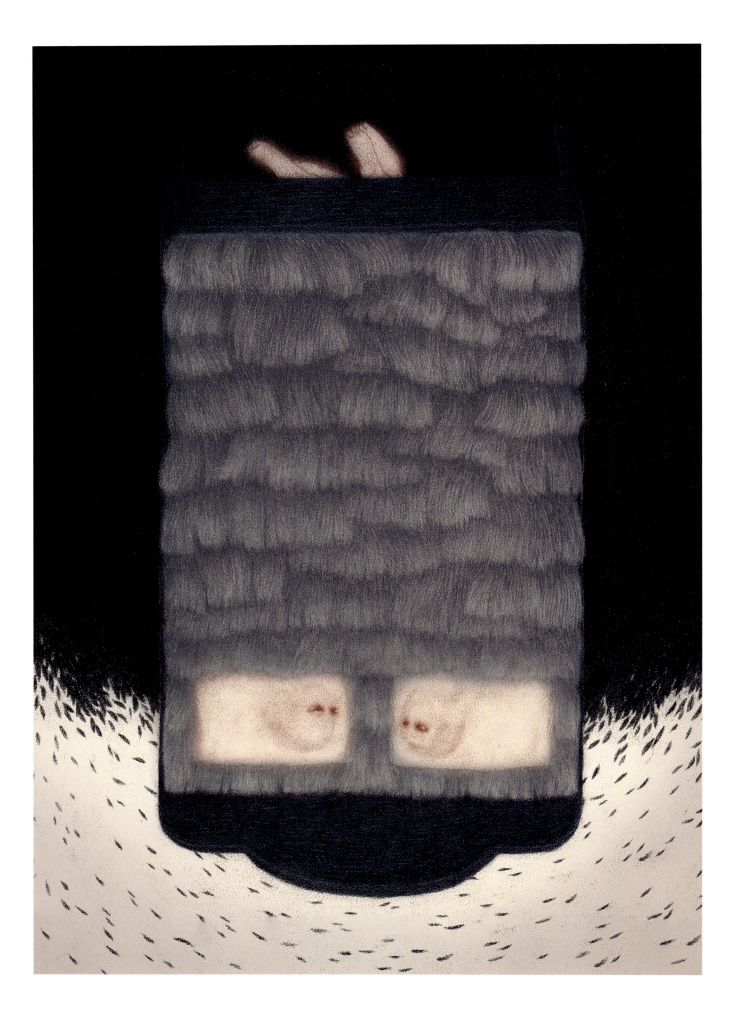

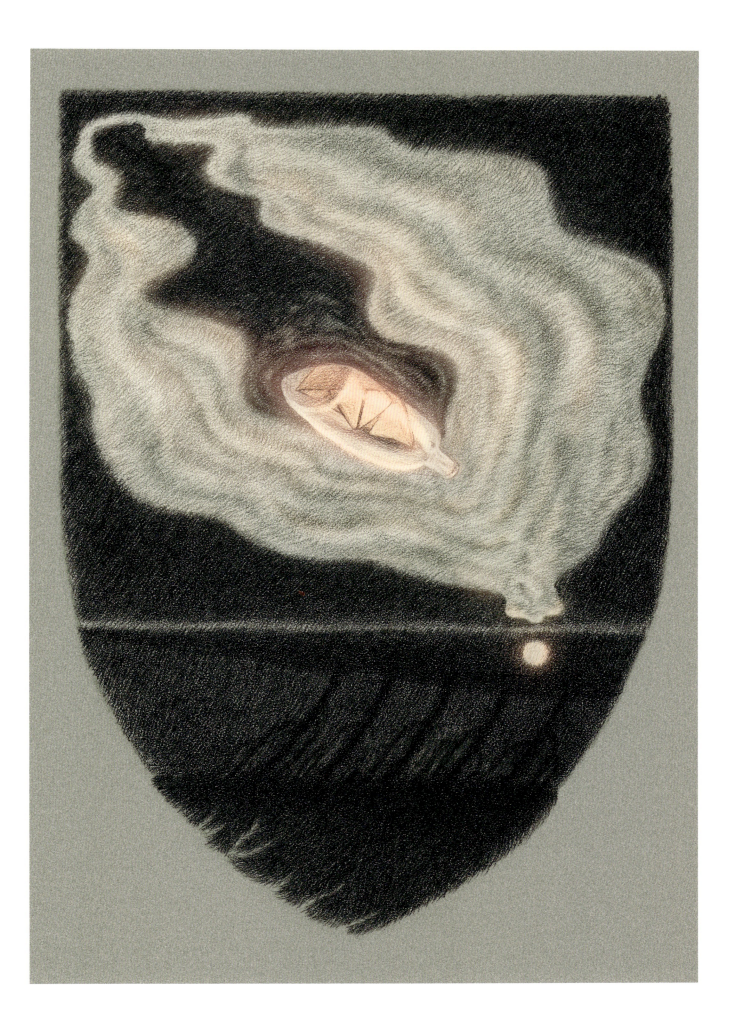

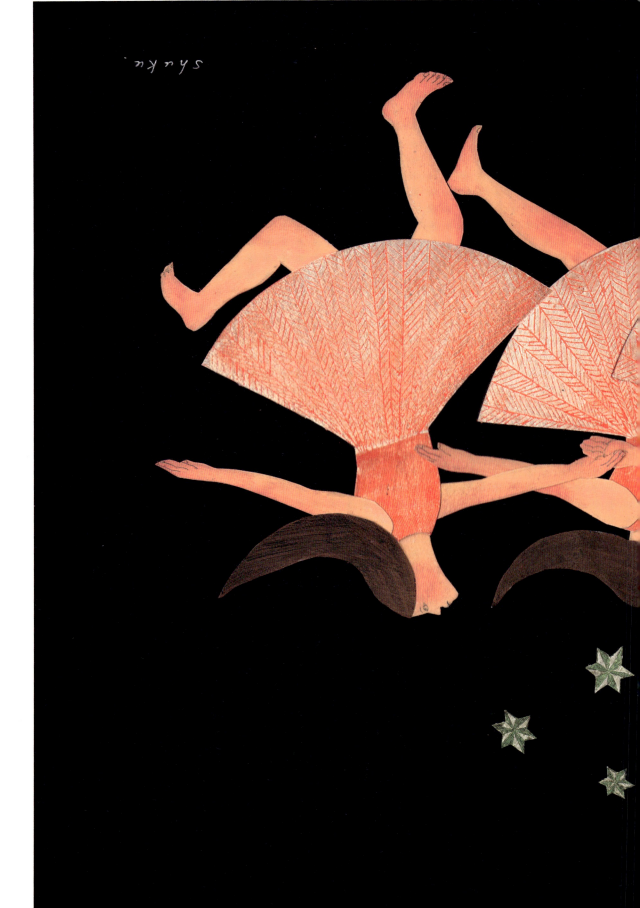

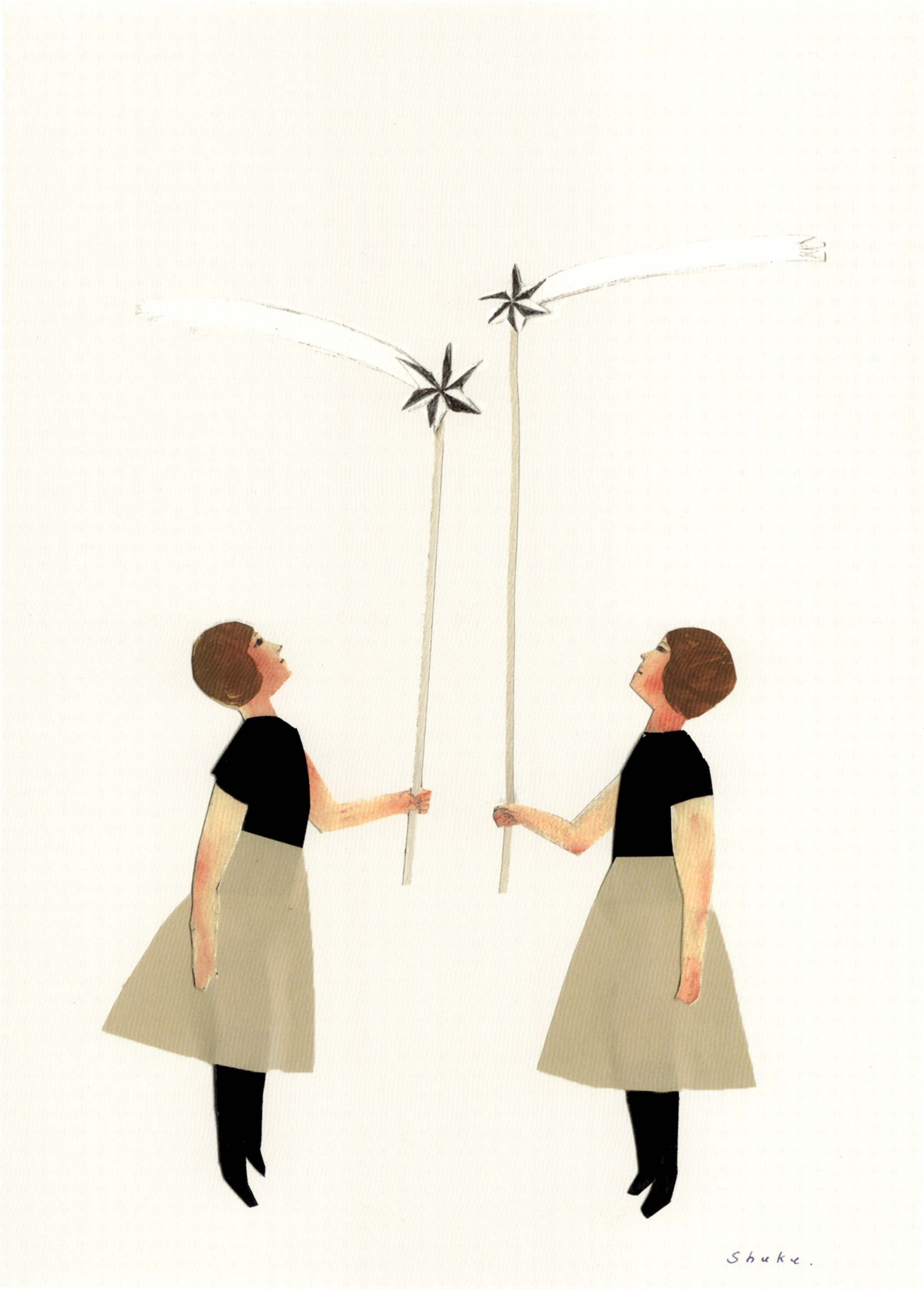
Shuku.

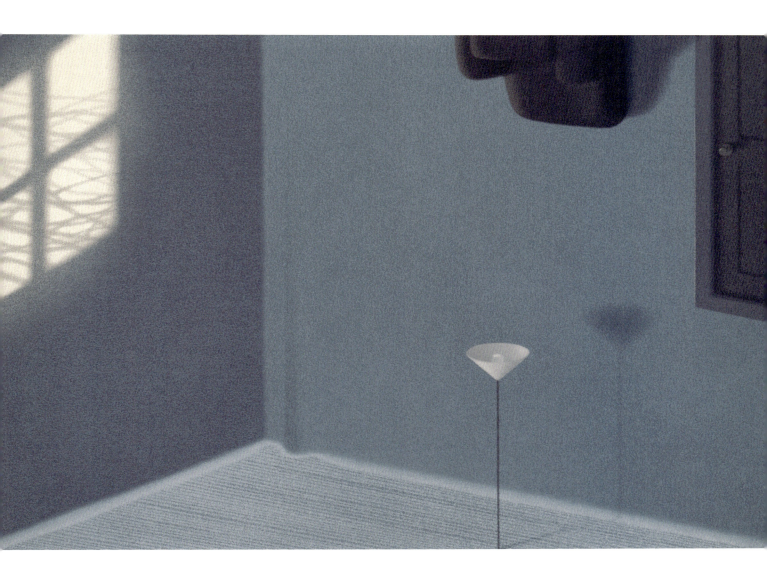

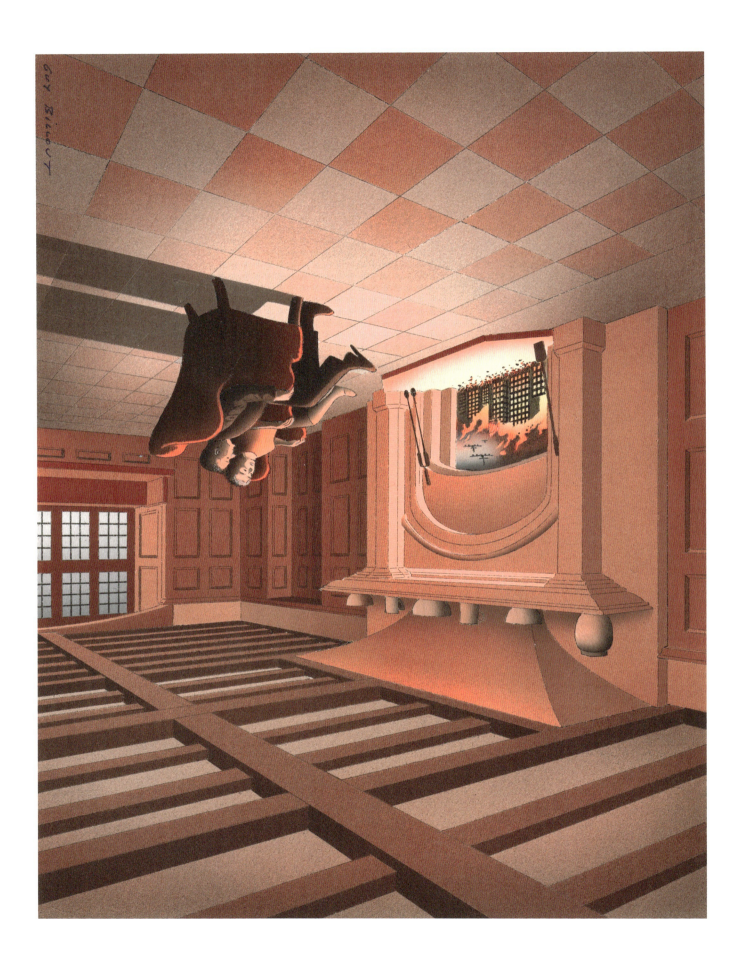

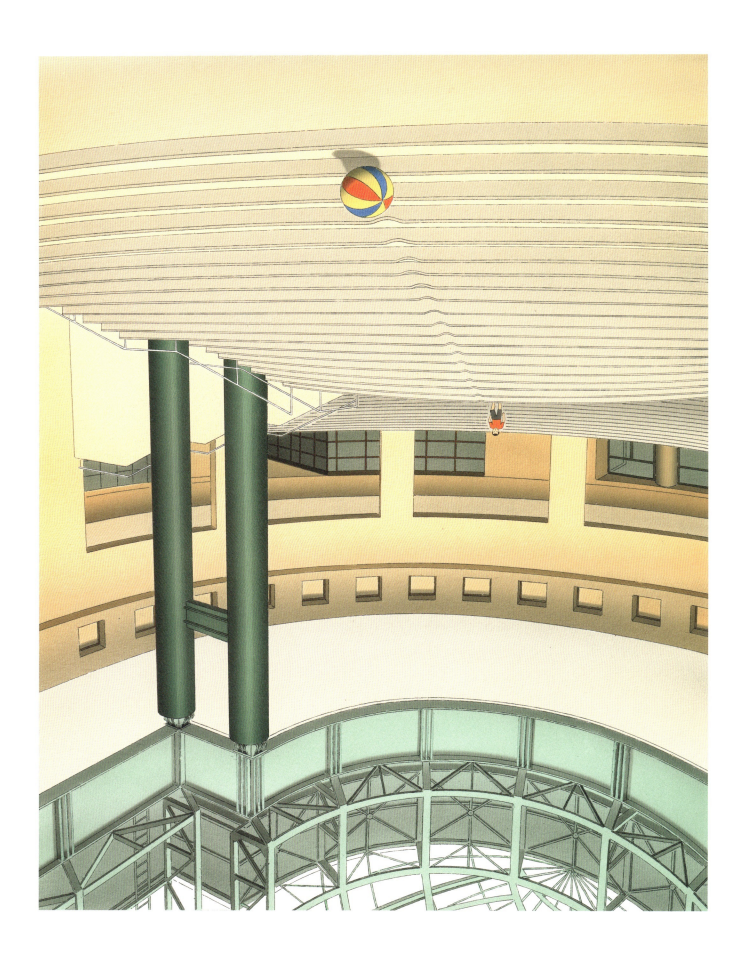

A SIMPLE GUIDE TO GETTING LOST IN REVERIE

In this book, you will not find a Table of Contents nor page numbers, for—much like the Cheshire Cat's response to Alice who asks him for directions in Wonderland—where you end up really does not matter.

All you have to do is follow your instincts INTO THE LIGHT or INTO THE DARK, and see where the dreams take you, as you wander through the surrealistic realms of the artists and illustrators featured.

BEFORE SETTING OFF, WE RECOMMEND...

(1) setting ample time aside for your thoughts to flow freely;
(2) preparing plenty of snacks or your favourite tea; and
(3) finding a cosy spot and a cat of your own for company.

Here's to the joy of discovering destinations unknown and losing yourself in the magic of the journey.

"Would you tell me, please,
which way I ought to go from here?"

"That depends a good deal on
where you want to get to,"
said the Cat.

"I don't much care where—"
said Alice.

"Then it doesn't matter
which way you go," said the Cat.

— Excerpt from 'Alice's Adventures in Wonderland'
by Lewis Carroll

As a child, I would often hear my mother say—half-reproachfully, half-indulgently—that I was 'on the moon,' a delightful expression in the French language that typically describes a person lost in reverie.

And—all by myself with no one around to tell me what to do—it was indeed a delightful place to be.

Growing up, although things did not change in that regard, I learned to take advantage of my role as an artist for legitimate reasons to live in the clouds; to daydream.

In writing this foreword about reveries, I decided to seek out their meaning, which originates from the ancient French word *rêverie*. Of the many definitions I came across, I was most drawn to the one that explains it as 'a mental activity not directed by rational thinking, but inspired by subjective and whimsical musing;

This discovery has helped me to make sense of my observations in the course of my illustration work so far, whether the assignments came with a theme, text written by somebody else, or total freedom.

With a given theme, I usually labour in search of a visual concept that illuminates or elucidates it – an often-agonising process that is mostly driven by arduous conscious thinking, and marred by the fear of not succeeding in finding the 'right' idea.

By contrast, when I am left to my own devices, I allow myself to be truly lost in reverie, with no fear of being inaccurate in my thinking, A good example of this occurred when The Atlantic Monthly magazine proposed that

I create a series of illustrations as a regular feature — with total editorial freedom.

The principle of this series was to depict a very precise, realistic scene, then adding a detail that 'derailed' that reality.

To this end, as a main source of inspiration, I relied on my own photographs, which I still shoot regularly with no specific purpose or topic in mind.

Looking at these random photos, I allowed myself to follow an unhindered train of thought until I found an idea that satisfied me, proceeding with its execution and—interestingly—entitling the visual *after* it was created.

This process is opposite to the one that takes place when I am given a title or text first, before starting work on a visual solution.

The act of trusting free-floating ideas and free associations that characterise a reverie generates a distinct kind of inspiration with a poetic dimension that I rarely attain when working for others' stories.

It underlines my experience writing children's books, in that I may not always know what I am doing at the beginning, but by just drawing and improvising, little by little things organise themselves.

Even after all these years, my mother, in her infinite wisdom, could never have imagined that her ineffectual son would develop the ability to make a living being 'on the moon.'

However, in the words of the great French author Victor Hugo: "Thought is the labour of the intellect, reverie is its pleasure."

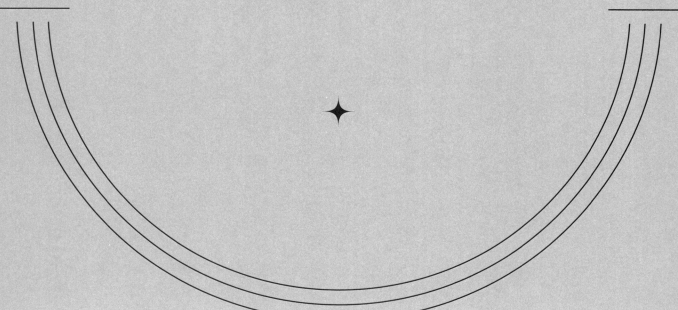

LOST IN REVERIE

FOREWORD
by GUY BILLOUT

LIGHT

INTO THE

LOST IN REVERIE
ART & ILLUSTRATION INSPIRED BY DREAMS

First published and distributed by
viction:workshop ltd.

viction:ary™

viction:workshop ltd.
Unit C, 7/F, Seabright Plaza,
9-23 Shell Street, North Point, Hong Kong

Url: viction:ary.com
Email: we@victionary.com
🌀 @victionworkshop
📷 @victionworkshop
🦄 @victionary
🌀 @victionary

Edited & produced by viction:ary

Cover images by Po-Hsun Huang & Marie Muravski
Creative direction by Victor Cheung
Book design by viction:workshop ltd.

ISBN 978-988-79727-2-3
Printed and bound in China

LOST IN REVERIE

LOST IN REVERIE

LOST IN REVERIE

LOST IN REVERIE

AKIRA KUSAKA · CHING-YAN LAI · DANIEL LIÉVANO · FUCO UEDA
GUY BILLOUT · HEATHER SUNDQUIST HALL · HOI CHAN · JUNCHO LEE
PEI-HSIN CHO · PETRA ERIKSSON · PHANTASIEN · PO-HSUN HUANG
RUNE FISKER · SHUKU NISHI · VICKI LING · WHOOLI CHEN